Building a House

by Byron Barton

 TeachingStrategies™ · Washington, DC

Buiding a House. Copyright © 1981 by Byron Barton. Published by
Teaching Strategies, Inc. by arragement with HarperCollins
Children's Books, a division of HarperCollins Publishers.
All rights reserved.

ISBN 978-1-60617-206-3

CPSIA tracking label information: RR Donnelley, Shenzhen,
China Date of Production: March 2012 Cohort: Batch 2
Printed and bound in China

3 4 5	14 13 12
Printing	Year Printed

THE LIBRARY OF CONGRESS HAS CATALOGED
THE HARPER COLLINS EDITION AS FOLLOWS:

Library of Congress Cataloging-in-Publication Data:
Barton, Byron. Building a house. "Greenwillow Books."
Summary: Briefly describes the steps in building a house.
1. House construction—Juvenile literature.   [1. House
construction.] I. Title. TH4811.5.B37690'.8373 80-22674

On a green hill

a machine digs a big hole.

Builders hammer and saw.

A cement mixer pours cement.

Bricklayers lay large white blocks.

Carpenters come and make a wooden floor.

They put up walls.

They build a roof.

A bricklayer builds a fireplace and a chimney too.

A plumber puts in pipes for water.

An electrician wires for electric lights.

Carpenters put in windows and doors.

Painters paint inside and out.

The workers leave.

The house is built.

The family moves inside.